GW01180223

THE GREEKS

Text: **Tom Stanier** and **Harry Sutton**
Illustrations: **Joseph McEwen**
Adviser: **Patsy Vanags**

BBC Publications in association with Heritage Books

Phidias the sculptor

Phidias was a famous sculptor who lived more than two thousand years ago. On these two pages you can see Phidias at home with his family and friends.
He has arranged a 'symposion', which was a drinking party for men. Phidias is greeting his guests as they arrive while the rest of his household make last minute preparations.
Phidias was a real person. Nobody knows about his family but one has been given to him in this book to make a story.

1 This is the chief guest. His name is Pericles and he is the most important man in Athens. Pericles has started a big building programme in the city.

2 This is Phidias. Pericles has put him in charge of the building construction. He is a famous sculptor and is making a statue for a new temple in honour of Athene, the patron goddess of Athens.

4 This is Charmides, the son of Phidias. He is nine years old, and one day will be a sculptor like his father.

3 This is Penelope, the wife of Phidias. She has made sure that all is ready for the symposion, but she will not be at the party. Women led separate lives in ancient Greece and she will spend the evening in the part of the house set aside for the women and children.

5 These are Chloe and Ismene, Charmide's sisters. Ismene is 15 years old and is soon to marry a 30-year-old man chosen for her by her father. Chloe is seven years old.

a entrance
b open courtyard
c well
d dining hall

e household altar
f bedroom
g kitchen

Charmides has a holiday

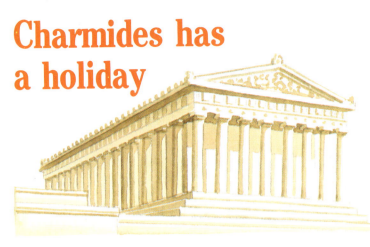

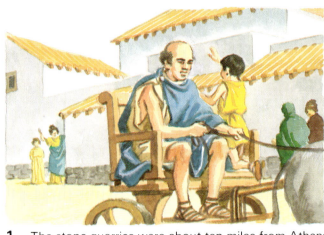

One day, Phidias took his son, Charmides, to see the stone quarries at Mount Pentelicus, near Athens. Afterwards, he showed him the temple he was working on for Pericles. On these two pages you can see where they went and what they saw.

1 The stone quarries were about ten miles from Athens so they had to go there in the family cart. There were not many roads in Greece at this time but one had been built to Pentelicus so that stone could be got to Athens.

2 On the way to the quarry they had to make way for a team of oxen pulling a cart loaded with stone; the cart had four wheels with wide treads.

3 Phideas was visiting the quarries to choose marble for the temple of Athena. While he was discussing the order with the master stone mason, Charmides asked one of the workmen to show him how stone was cut from the quarry. 'We first make holes in the stone, like this,' the mason told him . . .

4 . . . and then we fit wooden wedges into the holes. We pour water on to the wedges so that they swell and split the stone . . .

5 . . . along the natural line of the stone bed. Then we lever the stone out.

6 Phidias ordered marble for columns which would support the roof of the temple. The master mason showed him some blocks of stone being roughly shaped into sections of columns.
'Excellent,' said Phidias, and he gave him a sheet of papyrus (a kind of paper), with the sizes he needed.

7 Phidias was in a hurry to return to Athens for he was to meet Pericles at the new temple to be called the Parthenon. It was being built on the Acropolis (Greek for 'city on the hill').
They were nearly back to Athens when their way was blocked by an overturned cart. It was carrying timber for the roof of the temple.

8 When, at last, they reached the top of the Acropolis, Pericles was waiting for them. He was with some of the city officials. Actinus, who was the architect of the temple, greeted Phidias.
'You are just in time to show our city visitors the wonderful statue you are making of Athene,' he told him.

9 On the way to see the statue, they stopped to see one of the great marble columns being assembled. 'The marble is cut and smoothed so that the blocks fit perfectly together without any need for cement,' Actinus explained. 'Wooden pegs are used to centre them.'

10 In Phidias's workshop they saw the statue of the goddess Athene. It was more than 12 metres high and plated with gold and ivory. Pericles was very pleased with it. 'One day,' he told Charmides, 'perhaps you will be a famous sculptor like your father!'

Shopping in Athens

The busiest place in Athens was the 'Agora'. This was the market place where farmers sold their vegetables and where all the craftsmen and merchants of the city could display their goods. It was the centre of Athens and the place where people met to discuss the day's news.

1 Here you can see Penelope and Ismene out shopping. Their slaves do the bargaining for them. Their main foods were: wheat for bread, oatmeal for porridge, cheese, olives, eggs, fruit, fish, and vegetables. They would eat meat on festive days and they drank wine mixed with water.

2 Here is Charmides with his personal slave, Cimon. He is on his way to school and has stopped on the way to enjoy the noise and bustle of the Agora. Cimon is responsible for his young master's safety and good behaviour. He will soon move him on for otherwise he will be late for school.

3 This building was called a 'stoa' and was a covered place where people could meet, out of the heat or cold.

4 These young men are returning from an all-night symposion. They have had a little too much to drink and are being hustled away by two policemen.
The police in Athens were slaves from South Russia and were famous archers.

5 These are slaves for sale. They were well treated and were paid for their work in Athens. Many bought themselves out of slavery and became freemen.

6 This is Herodotus, the famous historian who has come to recite his history to the people of Athens. He hopes that they will pay him so that he can go on writing history. He is now telling the people about his lectures and how much they must pay to listen. Charmides is wondering whether his father will let him go and listen to Herodotus.

Other things to look for in the picture are:

7 Pottery for sale
8 A shoemaker and his wares
9 A merchant and his slaves
10 Soldiers
11 Statues of Athenian heroes
12 Public notice board
13 Office of weights and measures
14 Council chamber
15 Temple of Hephaites

Charmides at school

Only boys went to school in ancient Greece. The girls were taught to play musical instruments and to dance. They learned about housekeeping and how to spin and weave. They did learn to read and write but it was considered more important for boys to have proper schooling. On these two pages you can see what Charmides learned at school.

1 Cimon the slave persuaded Charmides at last, to stop loitering in the Agora and they joined up with other pupils to walk to school. These, of course, were the sons of quite rich parents who could afford to pay school fees. The sons of poor people could not go to school at all.

2 The schoolhouse was quite small. The slaves who looked after the boys were old servants who had become part of the family. Many of these slaves could read and write and children learned much wisdom from them.

3 The first lesson was writing. This was done on wax-coated tablets using a sharp-pointed instrument called a 'stylus'. The other end of the stylus was flattened so that mistakes could be smoothed out on the wax.

4 The teaching of good behaviour was an important part of Greek schooling and the teachers were very strict. A lesson badly done would bring certain punishment!

5 The Greeks loved music and all the boys at the school were taught to play an instrument and to sing. Charmides was learning to play the lyre. The other instruments being taught are double pipes.

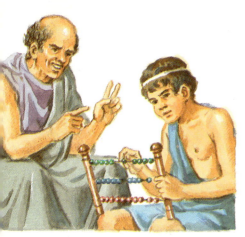

6 The next lesson was arithmetic which the Greeks did on a frame with beads called an 'abacus'. Addition, multiplication and subtraction could all be done on the abacus. It was a very good system which is still used in China and a few other countries.

7 It was now time for a break from work. The boys on the right played 'knuckle-bones', which were the ankle bones of goats or sheep. Five bones had to be thrown in the air and as many as possible caught on the back of the hand. It was hard to do. Try it with small pebbles or nuts.

8 Outdoor exercise, to make the body healthy and strong, was important in Greek schools. Every boy hoped that one day he might compete at the games held every fourth year at Olympia (see the map at the front of the book). The Olympic games are, of course, still held every four years but now they take place in a different country each time.

9 Although the Greeks could read and write, printing had not been invented and most knowledge, therefore, had to be passed from one generation to the next by word of mouth. A good memory was very important and boys were taught at school to memorise complete stories. Charmides has been called before the class to recite a favourite Greek story. It is the myth of Jason and the Argonauts and how they set sail to find the Golden Fleece.

JASON AND THE GOLDEN FLEECE

A long time ago, in the country of Thessaly, there lived two children. A boy called Phrixus and his sister Helle. Some would have said they were lucky children for their father was a king. Not only that, they had been befriended by the young god, Hermes, and he had given them a pet ram to play with — a wonderful ram with a fleece of gold.

But all was not well. For there was one person in the palace who did not love the children. Ino, their wicked stepmother, was jealous of Phrixus and Helle and secretly she plotted their deaths.

Now it so happened that no rain had fallen that summer. Month after month the sun scorched down and nothing would grow. Ino saw her chance. 'My lord,' she said to the king, 'the gods must be punishing us. Let me send to Delphi. The oracle will

A month later, the messengers returned and were summoned before the king. 'Well,' said the king, 'what says the oracle?' 'We bring sad tidings,' said the messengers. 'If the rains are to return, an offering must be made. Phrixus and Helle, your two children, must be sacrificed to the gods.'

Sorrowfully, the king led his children to the altar where they would be slain. But, just as they approached the temple, something extraordinary happened. The ram stopped, and it seemed to Phrixus and Helle that a voice was talking to them — very quietly so that no one else could hear. 'Climb on to my back', said the voice, 'and hold tight to my fleece.'

The children did as they were told, and suddenly the ram rose into the air and flew away, high above the people's heads, carrying them to safety.

On and on the ram flew, and below them they saw the sea and islands, white towers and temples, fields and ships. The children began to grow tired. 'Hold on,' said the ram, 'we shall soon be there.'

Phrixus tightened his grip on the fleece and held on grimly, but poor Helle became sleepier and sleepier. Finally, her eyes closed in sleep, and she let go of the ram.

Down she fell, down, down, to the sea. The waters closed over her, and the place where she was drowned is named after her to this day — the Hellespont.

Meanwhile, Phrixus and the ram flew on until they came at last to the country of Colchis, by the Black Sea. The long journey was over and one of the children had lived to tell the tale.

tell us what to do. The oracle always knows.'

'Very well, Ino,' said the king, 'go and consult her. I will do anything she tells me to do.' Ino laughed to herself for her plan was working. Then she called two of her servants to her. 'Go to Delphi and consult the oracle,' she told them, 'but then forget her words. Wipe them from your minds and when you return here I shall tell you what to say to the king.'

The ram, however, was so tired and wearied by the long journey that it fell down and died. When the people of Colchis heard what had happened to the miraculous ram, they decided to honour its memory. They stripped off its golden fleece and hung it on a tree in the wood. Then, so that no thief could ever steal the fleece, they set a monstrous dragon to guard it.

The years went by. Phrixus grew up into a man, and then he in turn became old, and died.

Meanwhile, back in Greece another young hero was growing up. His name was Jason and he was of royal blood. By rights he should have been the next king of Iolchos, but his wicked uncle had seized the throne for himself. And for his own protection, Jason's friends had sent him away to the mountains where his uncle could not reach him.

There Jason spent his youth, but when he was fully grown he set off back to Iolchis to claim his throne.

After he had journeyed for two days, he came to a river in flood. He was about to leap in and swim across when he heard a voice. It was an old woman. 'Help me,' she cried, 'the current is strong and I am old and weak. Will you carry me across?'

'Gladly,' said Jason. Then, lifting her up he bore her across the flooded river. He had to struggle hard and in the course of crossing he lost one of his sandals in the water. But in the end they came safely across and Jason set the old woman down. 'You have done well today,' said the old woman. Then, quite suddenly, she vanished.

This was no ordinary old woman.

It was Hera, queen of the Gods who had disguised herself to test Jason — and he had proved himself worthy of her protection. From this day forth, the gods would go with him.

Jason continued on his journey down to the city and went straight to the palace.

'I have come to see Pelias,' he said to the guards, and he was shown in to the king.

When Pelias saw Jason, he turned white with terror. It had been prophesised long ago that he would lose his throne to a man who wore only one sandal. And the first thing he noticed about Jason was that he had one foot bare!

'Who are you?' he asked, fearfully.

'I am Jason, your nephew whom you thought dead, and I have come to claim my rightful throne.'

Now Pelias was as cunning as he was cowardly.

'Gladly will I surrender my throne,' he said, 'for it is a wearisome business to rule. There is a curse on this country and the curse will not be lifted until the Golden Fleece of Phrixus is brought back to us. If you are strong enough to bring back the Fleece, then you are strong enough to be king. Will you do it?'

Without hesitation, Jason left the palace and began his preparations. And Pelias, the wily king, watched him go with a crooked smile on his lips, for he believed that Jason was going to his doom.

News spread fast of Jason's brave mission and young men flocked to join him. This was their chance for glory and adventure. Together they built a fine new ship. The hills all around rang to the sound of their axes as they worked. They named their vessel the Argo and Jason called his company of men the 'Argonauts'. In three months they were ready and one fine morning, they set sail for Colchis.

It was a journey that was to take many months. On the way they put in at an island to take on more stores. The king of the island was a blind man called Phineus, who led a wretched life. Not only was he blind, but he was persecuted by some flying monsters called Harpies. Evil smelling creatures, ugly and horrible! So greedy were they that whenever food was put on the table for King Phineus, they swooped down and seized it for themselves. Poor Phineus had not had a proper meal for years.

The Argonauts were shocked at his plight and promised to chase the Harpies away. A banquet was laid for the King and they settled down to wait. Sure enough, in a matter of minutes, the Harpies arrived and swooped down, screeching their horrible cries. But this time they were in for a nasty surprise. They were met by a hail of arrows from the Argonauts, and they flew away in terror, never to return again.

Phineus thanked Jason from the bottom of his heart and to repay the Argonauts for their services, he told them the secret of the Clashing Rocks . . .

'To reach Colchis,' he told them, 'you will have to sail between two giant rocks which every now and then, clash together and crush whatever is passing through. When you arrive at these rocks, here is what you must do. Release a white pigeon. If it flies safely through, that is a sign that the gods are with you and will protect you. But if the pigeon is crushed by the rocks, you too are doomed'.

The Argonauts thanked the old man and sailed away. On they travelled, day after day, until one morning they heard a rumbling like distant thunder.

It was the Clashing Rocks, and as they drew closer they saw them rising out of the sea like two gigantic teeth. Even as they watched, they saw the two rocks smash thunderously together.

'We must turn back!' cried the Argonauts.

'No!' Jason told them. 'We must trust in Phineus. Release the pigeon.'

The Argonauts watched anxiously as the bird flew towards the narrow gap. It flew straight as an arrow. Hungrily the rocks began to close like the jaws of a wild beast — and the bird was swallowed up.

Or so it seemed.

But when the rocks opened up again, a great shout rose from the Argonauts — for there was the pigeon, flying safely away on the other side.

'Row!', cried Jason. 'Row men, row as you have never rowed before!'

The sea boiled beneath their oars, and, next minute, the Argo too had shot safely through the gap — only a fraction of a second before the jagged black rocks clashed together again.'

They were safe, and before them lay the open sea.

After many more adventures they finally reached their destination and when they arrived at Colchis they were met by King Aetes. He greeted them and asked them their business.

'We have come to bring back the Golden Fleece,' Jason told him. 'There is a curse on the land of Iolchos which will never be lifted unless the Fleece is returned to us.'

King Aetes trembled with anger and he was determined to send this bold young stranger to his doom.

'You shall have the Fleece,' he said, 'but only if you can prove yourself a better man than me. Tomorrow you must yoke the fire-breathing bulls; then you must sow the Sacred Field of Ares with dragons' teeth; and then you must kill the guardian serpent. Do that, and you may have the Fleece.'

'I accept your challenge,' said Jason. And he turned away to prepare himself for the fearsome task.

Aetes laughed to himself for he knew that the things he had demanded were impossible. But, unknown to him, his daughter Medea had fallen in love with the handsome stranger. She was a sorceress, gifted with magic powers, and that night she came to Jason with a magic ointment made from secret herbs.

'Rub it on yourself,' she told him, 'and it will protect you from the flames of the bulls. Otherwise you will be burnt to death. And when you have sown the dragons' teeth, throw a stone into the middle of the crops that grow there. Remember — throw a stone, or you will certainly die!'

The next morning, the Greeks and the people of Colchis gathered at the field of Ares. As Jason approached the bulls, the crowd watched fearfully. It seemed that he must be scorched to death by their fiery breath — but the flames licked harmlessly about him.

He was untouched.

Then, as he spoke soothing words to them, the anger of the bulls seemed to die away and they allowed Jason to yoke them to the plough and drive them up and down the field. Thus was the first of the tasks done.

Jason now picked up the bag of dragons' teeth and strode up and down the furrows, sowing the teeth as he went. 'This is easy enough,' he said to himself. 'This is child's play!' But he was wrong, for after he had finished the sowing, a crop began to grow. And it was not green corn that sprouted forth — but a crop of fully armed soldiers!

Jason gazed in astonishment. And his astonishment soon turned to fear, for the soldiers pointed their spears threateningly at Jason and prepared to advance on him. Jason was trapped. How could he fight an army, unarmed and single handed? But then he remembered Medea's advice.

He picked up a rock and hurled it through the air so that it landed near the rear of the armed men and struck one of the soldiers. From where he had been standing, the soldier could not see where the stone had come from; he thought it had been thrown by one of his companions and, leaping to his feet he struck out at the nearest man.

In hitting back, the second man struck his neighbour a blow. Instantly, his neighbour struck out in his turn, and soon a fierce battle had begun.

All Jason had to do was to stand back and watch as his enemies slaughter each other to the last man.

King Aetes was furious, but he pretended to admire the young Greek's courage.

'Well done, Jason,' he told him. 'You are a brave man and a clever one. Tomorrow you shall have the Fleece.'

Jason was triumphant. He had won. But that night, Medea came to him with bad news.

'My father's word is not to be trusted,' she told Jason. 'He means to kill you tomorrow and he will kill me too, for he knows that it was I who helped you. This is what you must now do. Rouse your men and tell them to make ready to sail — but do it secretly. Meanwhile, you and I will fetch the Fleece — now, by dead of night.'

So, while the Argonauts hurried stealthily down to their ship, Jason and Medea went off into the woods. It was pitch dark but Medea knew the tracks of the forest and they arrived safely at a clearing. On a tree, was the Golden Fleece, shining through the night with a mysterious glow. And there below it, was a gigantic guardian dragon.

It was a fearful monster and even Jason started back in horror. But the magic of Medea was equal to the task. Muttering secret spells, she sprinkled special herbs in front of the dragon. Its forked tongue licked them up and in a moment, it was fast asleep.

Instantly, Jason plucked down the Fleece and they hurried triumphantly back to their ship.

An hour later, as dawn began to break, the Argonauts rowed with muffled oars away from Colchis.

The Fleece was theirs. The task was done. And now Jason could return to claim his rightful throne.

Herodotus and the wars with Persia

When Charmides returned from school, he told his father about seeing Herodotus in the agora. 'He is going to recite in the gymnasium,' he told him. 'Can Cimon take me to hear him?' 'Well', said Phidias, 'if I let you go, you must listen carefully and tell me afterwards all that you have heard, for Herodotus tells the story of our most famous days — when the Greeks stood alone against the might of Persia.' Charmides promised to listen well and the next day he went off with Cimon to the recitation. (You can find the places Herodotus mentioned in his lecture on the map inside the front cover.)

1 'When our story starts,' said Herodotus, 'Persia was the greatest power on earth…

2 The man who wielded that power was the Great King Darius. He ruled an empire that stretched from India to the Black Sea.

3 For many years, young Greeks had been leaving home to start new lives abroad, in the lands ruled by Persia. The Greeks in one of these places rebelled against the laws of King Darius. To help them, the Athenians sent an army which attacked and burned the city of Sardis, in Ionia.

4 When the Great King heard about the burning of Sardis, he called for a bow and an arrow. Firing the arrow into the air, he cried: 'Grant, O God, that I may punish the Athenians!' Then he commanded one of his servants to repeat the words: 'Master, remember the Athenians', three times whenever he sat down to dinner.

5 In the year 490 BC, the Great King Darius decided to take his revenge and he sent an army of more than 25,000 men in 400 ships, to attack and destroy Athens. The Persians landed on a beach at Marathon, only 40 kms from the city.

6 To the south of Athens, there lived a warlike people, trained from childhood to be soldiers. These were the Spartans, and when the news came of the Persian landings, a fast runner named Pheidippides was sent to Sparta to ask for help.

7 From Athens to Sparta was 225 kms and Pheidippides ran all night and all day without stopping. He reached Sparta to find the Spartans celebrating a religious festival. 'We cannot come to the aid of Athens,' they told him, 'until after the full moon, which is in ten days' time.'

8 Meanwhile, not waiting for the Spartans, the Athenians marched against the enemy and a great battle was fought. The Greeks were outnumbered by more than two to one, but they were better armed than the Persians. They were also fighting for their own land whereas the Persian soldiers were in a foreign land, far from home.

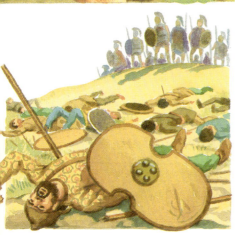

9 It was a great Athenian victory, and when at last the Spartans arrived, there was nothing left for them to do. The Persians had been defeated and those not killed had fled in their ships, back to Persia.

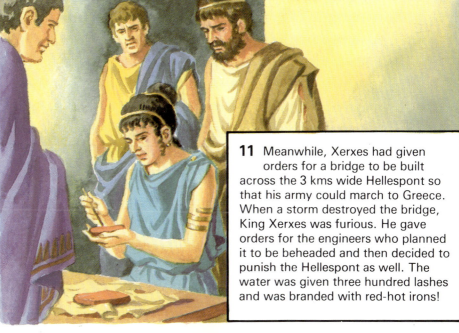

11 Meanwhile, Xerxes had given orders for a bridge to be built across the 3 kms wide Hellespont so that his army could march to Greece. When a storm destroyed the bridge, King Xerxes was furious. He gave orders for the engineers who planned it to be beheaded and then decided to punish the Hellespont as well. The water was given three hundred lashes and was branded with red-hot irons!

10 Ten years went by. King Darius was dead and a new king, Xerxes, planned a second invasion of Greece. He hoped to catch the Greeks unawares but they had a friend at the Persian court who sent them a secret message. It was on a set of wax tablets and at first the Greeks could not make sense of it. But then the queen of the Spartans found the secret. She scraped off the wax and there, underneath, was the vital message — telling them that the Persians were planning another attack.

12 A much stronger bridge was built and the army of the Great King began its long march to Greece.

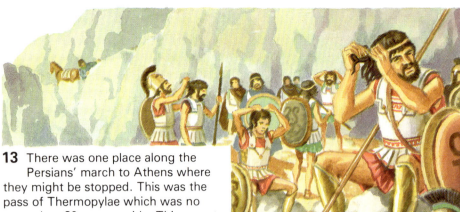

13 There was one place along the Persians' march to Athens where they might be stopped. This was the pass of Thermopylae which was no more than 20 metres wide. This meant that only a few soldiers in the huge Persian army would be able to fight at any one time. But Xerxes was not worried — particularly when a scout told him that he had seen Spartan soldiers combing their hair. Xerxes laughed scornfully — what kind of soldiers were these!

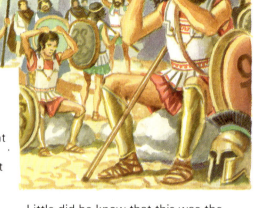

Little did he know that this was the custom of Spartan soldiers who were preparing to fight to the death.

14 The Great King sent his finest troops forward to break through the pass, but he had underestimated the Spartans. Time and again they thrust forward, and always the line held.

15 There seemed to be no way of breaking through the narrow pass, but then a Greek traitor named Ephialtes asked to see the king. 'I know a way round,' he told him. And that evening, Ephialtes led a strong force of Persians along a secret track which would take them behind the Greek position.

16 The leader of the Greeks in Thermopylae was Leonidas, King of the Spartans. When he got news of the Persian march to his rear, he made a brave decision. He told his allies to leave while they could. The Spartans would defend the pass alone.

17 Nothing frightened the Spartans — not even the news that the Persians shot arrows in such great volleys that they blotted out the sun. 'Excellent', said one Spartan soldier. 'In that case we shall be fighting in the shade and keep cool!'

18 It was a famous battle. King Leonidas had less than 2,000 men left, of whom 300 were Spartans. With these he stood defiant against 200,000 Persians and not one Spartan soldier was left alive. But their fame will live forever.

19 Delphi was the home of the famous oracle: the priestess of Apollo would go into a trance and speak messages from the god. Elders from Athens were now sent to ask the oracle how they should defend Athens from the Persians.

20 Athens had a new leader named Themistocles. When the oracle's message was given to him, he read it to the assembled people. 'The wooden walls shall not fail,' he read, 'but will help you and your children.' In that case, thought some people, when the Persians come to Athens, we should shut ourselves up inside the wooden walls of the city. Themistocles, however, persuaded them that the wooden walls were the wooden hulls of their warships. They must fight the Persians at sea.

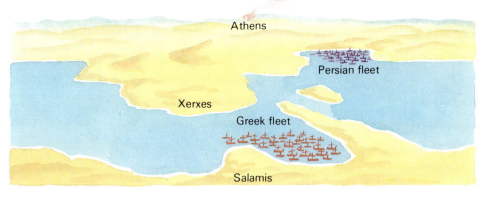

Athens

Persian fleet

Xerxes

Greek fleet

Salamis

21 It was decided that Athens should not be defended and that everybody too old or too young to fight, should leave the city and take refuge in the island of Salamis until the war was over.

22 The Greek women and children, safe on the island, watched as their own fleet of warships gathered along the Salamis coast. In the distance, they could see Athens burning as the Great King Xerxes took his long promised revenge. Then, to the east, they saw the Persian fleet. The great battle for the survival of Greece was about to start.

23 For several days, neither side made a move. Then Themistocles set a trap for the Persians. He gave orders for all the Greek ships to sail according to a carefully made plan. First, some of the ships hoisted sail and moved off as though they wanted to escape. Then others set off and pretended to panic when they saw the Persian fleet. From his camp on the far side of the bay, the Great King fell into the trap. Believing that the

Greeks really were running away, he gave orders for his ships to attack.

24 This, of course, was exactly what Themistocles had planned. As the Persian ships raced into the narrow waters off Salamis, the Greeks suddenly turned on them. Driving hard at the Persians, the Greek rowers straining at their oars, the Athenian ships rammed the enemy and tore into their banks of oars.

26 'That was almost the end of the Persian wars,' said Herodotus. 'The Great King had to march back to Persia, for without a fleet, his army could not be fed. He left a small part of the army behind with orders to fight the Athenians again, but it was too late. They were beaten at one last battle at a place called Platea and then they too had to retreat from Greece. The war was won and Greece was saved.'

25 The Great King watched as his fleet turned and ran. Most of the ships were destroyed as they went, for they could not turn in the narrow waters and the Greeks rammed them as they tried to get away.

PERSEUS AND THE GORGONS

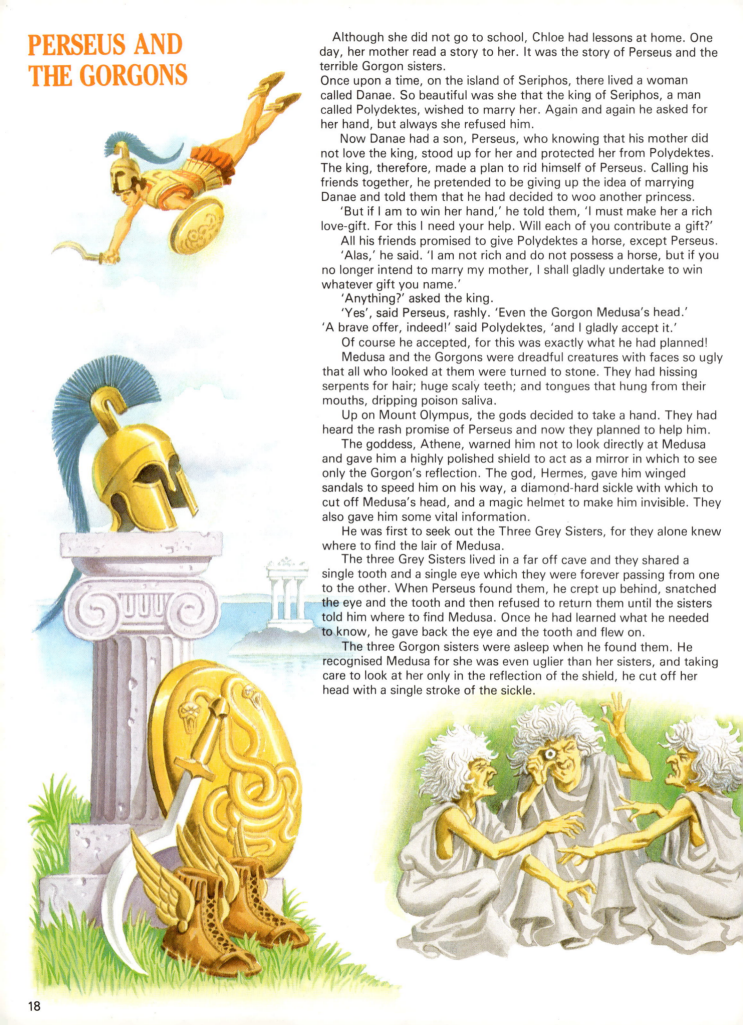

Although she did not go to school, Chloe had lessons at home. One day, her mother read a story to her. It was the story of Perseus and the terrible Gorgon sisters.

Once upon a time, on the island of Seriphos, there lived a woman called Danae. So beautiful was she that the king of Seriphos, a man called Polydektes, wished to marry her. Again and again he asked for her hand, but always she refused him.

Now Danae had a son, Perseus, who knowing that his mother did not love the king, stood up for her and protected her from Polydektes. The king, therefore, made a plan to rid himself of Perseus. Calling his friends together, he pretended to be giving up the idea of marrying Danae and told them that he had decided to woo another princess.

'But if I am to win her hand,' he told them, 'I must make her a rich love-gift. For this I need your help. Will each of you contribute a gift?'

All his friends promised to give Polydektes a horse, except Perseus.

'Alas,' he said. 'I am not rich and do not possess a horse, but if you no longer intend to marry my mother, I shall gladly undertake to win whatever gift you name.'

'Anything?' asked the king.

'Yes', said Perseus, rashly. 'Even the Gorgon Medusa's head.'

'A brave offer, indeed!' said Polydektes, 'and I gladly accept it.'

Of course he accepted, for this was exactly what he had planned!

Medusa and the Gorgons were dreadful creatures with faces so ugly that all who looked at them were turned to stone. They had hissing serpents for hair; huge scaly teeth; and tongues that hung from their mouths, dripping poison saliva.

Up on Mount Olympus, the gods decided to take a hand. They had heard the rash promise of Perseus and now they planned to help him.

The goddess, Athene, warned him not to look directly at Medusa and gave him a highly polished shield to act as a mirror in which to see only the Gorgon's reflection. The god, Hermes, gave him winged sandals to speed him on his way, a diamond-hard sickle with which to cut off Medusa's head, and a magic helmet to make him invisible. They also gave him some vital information.

He was first to seek out the Three Grey Sisters, for they alone knew where to find the lair of Medusa.

The three Grey Sisters lived in a far off cave and they shared a single tooth and a single eye which they were forever passing from one to the other. When Perseus found them, he crept up behind, snatched the eye and the tooth and then refused to return them until the sisters told him where to find Medusa. Once he had learned what he needed to know, he gave back the eye and the tooth and flew on.

The three Gorgon sisters were asleep when he found them. He recognised Medusa for she was even uglier than her sisters, and taking care to look at her only in the reflection of the shield, he cut off her head with a single stroke of the sickle.

He thrust the head into a bag and was just flying off when the other Gorgons awoke. Seeing Medusa dead, they tried to catch Perseus. Quickly, he put on the helmet and was at once invisible.

High above the sea on the long journey home, he happened to look down and saw a beautiful girl chained to a sea cliff. On the shore nearby there was a group of people, weeping and lamenting. When Perseus landed beside them, he was told that the girl's name was Andromeda and that she was the king's only daughter.

'Alas', they said. 'Now she is to be sacrificed to a fierce sea monster that has been terrorising our shores. The gods sent the monster and only her death will appease them.'

Perseus was horrified. He had fallen deeply in love with Andromeda at his first sight of her and now he told the people that he would rescue her if she would be his wife and return with him to Greece.

The king agreed to this at once, for he was grief-stricken that his beautiful daughter was to die. Suddenly a shout went up.

'The monster! The monster is coming!'

Swift as an arrow, Perseus flew out to sea and with one sweep of his sickle he cut off the monster's head. Moments later he had unfastened Andromeda's chains and carried her safely back to the shore.

Andromeda and Perseus were married and he took his wife home to Greece. There Perseus found that King Polydektes had made even stronger attempts to persuade Danae to be his wife. Perseus decided to punish the faithless king.

Going directly to the palace where Polydektes was feasting with his companions, Perseus took Medusa's head from the bag and held it up for all to see. Instantly the king and all his court were turned to stone.

Perseus turned to his mother.

'Live in peace,' he said. 'Your enemy will trouble you no more.'

The legacy of Greece

Legacy is the word we use to describe the things left behind by people when they die. It can also mean the things left behind by a whole civilisation: such things as laws, languages, ideas and inventions.

The whole world has benefitted from the ancient Greeks and in the next few pages you will see some of their legacies, handed down to us through the ages.

The Greek theatre

For the Greeks, Dionysus was the god of all living things and festivals were held in his honour. Plays were presented in theatres specially built on hillsides so that as many people as possible could see.

The theatre of Dionysus at Athens could seat about 14,000 people in tiered seats, and even bigger theatres were built elsewhere in Greece. On this page you can learn about what the Greeks saw when they went to the theatre at the festival of Dionysus.

1 The festival went on for several days and there were competitions to see who could write the best plays. As a rule, there were only three speaking actors who wore different masks to show what parts they were playing.

2 The action of plays took place in a circular area called the 'orchestra'. Behind it was a wooden building in which the actors changed their clothes.

3 Because they wore masks, the actors could not use facial expressions to show anger, pleasure, or other emotions.

The audience, in the open air, were set back a long way from the stage and the actors had to make sweeping gestures and speak very clearly so that everybody could hear and understand. The plays were written down so that the actors could learn their parts. Many Greek plays, first performed more than 2,000 years ago, have survived and are still performed from time to time, in modern theatres. This is one of the legacies we still enjoy from ancient Greece.

A Greek vase

The Greeks made beautiful pottery. Athens was especially famous for vases decorated with pictures of life in ancient times. It was usual for vases to be put into coffins when people died and large numbers of these, in perfect condition, have been dug up and can be seen in museums. The pictures on the vases and their beautiful shapes have inspired potters and artists ever since. They are another legacy that we have from ancient Greece.

Many vases were badly broken when they were found and archaeologists had to put the pieces carefully together. How good an archaeologist are you?
On this page there are 17 pieces of a broken vase. Trace on to a card the outlines and the parts of the pictures in each piece and then cut them out. See if you can fit them together to make the original vase. There is a picture of the complete vase inside the back cover.

Greek science and invention

In ancient times, most people did not question the things of nature they saw around them. They were too busy finding food and shelter to worry about *why* things happened. If things went wrong — if storms destroyed their crops or if their animals died of disease, they believed that the gods were angry and were punishing them.

The Greek scholars did not believe this and they thought seriously about the world. They tried to find explanations for the things they saw and on this page you can see some of the discoveries and inventions they made. They left them as legacies for other scholars and inventors, right up to modern times.

Medicine Greek doctors studied the human body by cutting open and examining bodies. They discovered that diseases are not caused by evil spirits, as primitive people believed. They found that there were natural causes for many illnesses and deaths.

The best known Greek doctor was Hippocrates. He taught his followers how to examine their patients and find out what was wrong with them. Modern doctors still respect the 'Hippocratic oath' by which they dedicate their lives to the care of their patients.

Astronomy.
Astronomy. Until Greek scholars began to study the stars, it was believed that the Earth was fixed in the middle of the universe and that the sun, moon and the stars revolved round it. A famous Greek mathematician called Pythagoras was the first to say that the earth was a sphere, hanging in space. He was right, and so were those of his

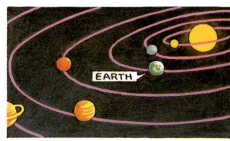

followers who came to believe that the earth revolved round its own axis.

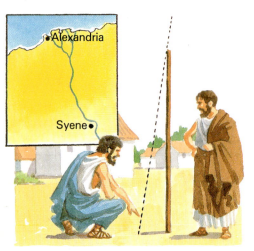

Mathematics.
Another Greek scholar, named Eratosthenes, measured the circumference of the earth to an accuracy of 320 kms. He knew the exact distance between Alexandria and Syene, two towns in Egypt, and when the sun was overhead in Syene, he measured its angle at Alexandria. Then, using mathematics, he got the answer almost exactly right — more than 2,000 years ago!

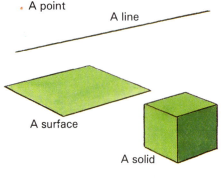

A point
A line
A surface
A solid

The ancient Egyptians had used simple arithmetic and geometry for many centuries to measure the lands irrigated by the Nile river floods. The Greeks took these ideas and built them into a science. The most famous Greek scholar of all was Euclid who invented geometry, the study of space. His books on geometry were the most successful text books ever written. Above you can see four different kinds of space that Euclid wrote about in his book.

Inventions One of the best known of Greek scientists and inventors was called Archimedes. He worked out one important idea in physics by thinking about the water level in his bath. he was so excited at finding the solution to the problem that he leapt out of the water and ran naked through the streets shouting: 'Eureka!' (I have discovered it!)

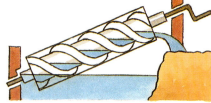

He also invented the Archimedes' screw — a device for raising water from one level to another which is still used. There are instructions for making a simple working model of Archimedes' screw on the page opposite.

Model of a Greek temple

You will need: Empty detergent packets; the inners of kitchen rolls, or toilet rolls; corrugated card.

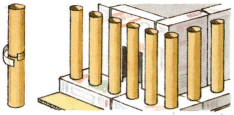

1   Glue empty detergent packets together like this. Glue them to the baseboard and to each other. This is the plinth of the temple.

2   Fit more detergent packets together like this. Glue them to each other and to the plinth. Cut a door into the temple in the front packet.

3   Glue kitchen roll inners (or toilet roll inners taped together) to the plinth, to make the columns.

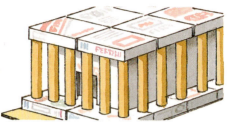

4   Glue more detergent packets to the tops of the columns to make the architrave. If you use toilet roll inners, you will need to fix squares of corrugated card to the base and top of each to make them tall enough.

5   Cut detergent packets in half diagonally, and glue the halves on top of the architrave to make the pediment and the roof supports.

6   Cut corrugated card and glue it in position to make the roof.

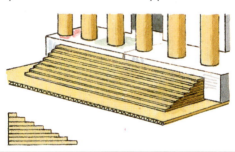

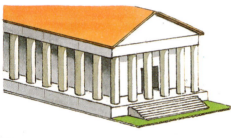

7   Cut strips of corrugated card, graded in width from 1 cm to 10 cms. Glue them together and to the baseboard to make steps up to the temple.

8   Paint the temple to make it look like this.

Model of Archimedes' water screw

You will need: A liquid detergent bottle; a length of ½-inch dowling; a wire coat hanger; a packet of Plasticine.

1   Cut the bottom off the detergent bottle and make two openings in the top like this. A sharp craft knife is needed to make these two openings so you may need help with it.

2   Cut a 12 cms length of dowling. Take a new packet of Plasticine and cut strips from it like this. Mould some Plasticine on to the rod to form a base for the screw.

3   Take more Plasticine and shape it round the rod to form a spiral. Test each spiral to see that it fits exactly inside the detergent bottle.

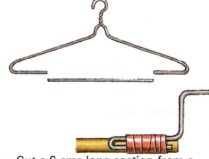

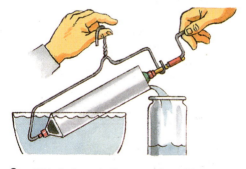

4   Push the spiral into the detergent bottle. Press dowling rod firmly down so that the end fits into the detergent bottle cap.

5   Cut a 6 cms long section from a wire coat hanger, like this. Bend it into a crank and fix the crank to the top of the dowling rod with sticky tape.

6   This is how it fits together. Turn the handle and water will be pumped out of the top of the water screw.

Guide to the Greek gods

Artemis. ▽
Goddess of hunting.

◁**Asclepius.**
God of medicine.

Hera. ▽
Wife of Zeus and queen of heaven.

△**Dionysus.**
God of wine.

Athene. △
Goddess of wisdom and of Athens.

Apollo. ▷
God of music, the arts, flocks and herds.

Pan. △
God of shepherds, huntsmen and country folk.

Demeter. ▷
Goddess of corn and of the earth.

Zeus. △
Lord of heaven and the father of all the gods and of men.

◁**Ares.**
God of war.

▽**Hades.**
God of the underworld.

Aphrodite. ▽
Goddess of love, daughter of Zeus and mother of Eros.

◁**Hermes.**
Messenger of Zeus and patron of travellers, shepherds, traders and robbers. The god who accompanied the dead to the other world.

Poseidon. △
King of the sea and god of horses.